CW00704816

Silver Link Silk Editions

SLP

One young lad's trainspotting trips with a camera, 1961-1964

Sixteen locos can be seen in this view of Annesley depot, most in steam and mainly waiting for their next freight duty. In the background can be seen some of the workings of Newstead Colliery. It was unusually quiet this Sunday, walking round the shed and only seeing one person and one car, presumably his (both on the extreme right of the photo), so I did not see a need to ask permission – I just wandered round. Top of the Pops that week was Mary Wells with *My Guy* – maybe he was that guy… (24 May 1964)

Silver Link Silk Editions

SLP

One young lad's trainspotting trips with a camera, 1961-1964

Alan M. Clarke

Silver Link Publishing Ltd

Dedication

To my wonderful loving wife Chris who fought cancer for the last 13 years, winning many battles on the way but finally losing the war on 22 January 2016. Miss you loads and you are in my thoughts for ever, love. Alan xxx

© Alan M. Clarke 2016

All rights reserved. No part of this publication may be reproduced, stored in a retrieval system or transmitted, in any form or by any means, electronic, mechanical, photocopying, recording or otherwise, without prior permission in writing from Silver Link Publishing Ltd.

First published in 2016

British Library Cataloguing in Publication Data

A catalogue record for this book is available from the British Library.

ISBN 978 1 85794 472 3

Silver Link Publishing Ltd
The Trundle
Ringstead Road
Great Addington
Kettering
Northants NN14 4BW

Tel/Fax: 01536 330588
email: sales@nostalgiacollection.com
Website: www.nostalgiacollection.com

Printed and bound in the Czech Republic

Contents

Front cover and title page: Un-named 'Deltic' No D9016 at Babworth Bridge, Retford, with an express from King's Cross in October 1963.

Introduction

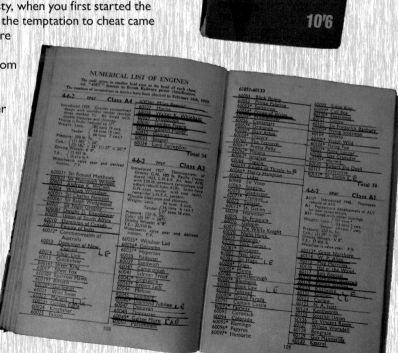

Hobbies – a disappearing word these days. Do kids really have hobbies any more? They have interests, but with technology their interests rapidly change and they move on to the next phase or generation electronically without leaving their seat!

Gone are the days of stamp, fag card, butterfly and coin collecting. These were the simple pastimes that kids could enjoy without the influence of the media. You could put your own interpretation on your pastime, and others enjoyed the same interests, so you were able to swop your duplicate items with friends. Always good with fag cards, as to get one Bobby Charlton you would probably have to give one Ron Springett, one Peter Swan and one David (Bronco) Layne (if you are not a Sheffield Wednesday fan, you will be saying 'Who the bloody hell are they?')

Also with that type of hobby you had some tangible evidence, i.e. a coin, cigarette card or stamp, as proof of your collection, but with a hobby like trainspotting it was really down to trust and honesty – you couldn't take a locomotive home, just the memory. Once you had seen a loco you would underline it in your Ian Allan abc Combined Volume, always looking to complete a set or class. This milestone eluded me –the nearest I got were the 'A4s', just missing one, No 60012 Commonwealth of Australia, and

the 'A1s', with No 60160 Auld Reekie. Both these were highly sought-after Scottish engines, which rarely came down to our Retford area, but having said that if you lived in Scotland they were easy sightings; our local common ones, say No 60025 Falcon or No 60114 W. P. Allen, were their prizes.

Going back to honesty, when you first started the hobby – and I was ten – the temptation to cheat came to everyone and I am sure most did it; for my sins I underlined 23 namers from classes 'B17', 'K2', 'D34', 'D11' and 'D49'. I can remember when another spotter was looking at my 'Combine' and asked where had I seen these Scottish engines, obviously noting that I had not seen many other Scottish ones in the 'Pacific' section, I replied, 'When I went to Blackpool – they were all on holiday specials.' I got away with it, but as you get older you know it is not the done thing, so I was about 12 when I put a red 'X' against these underlinings to put everything back on the straight and narrow.

I was introduced to the hobby in 1958, taking a short bus ride from Worksop to Retford at about 9 o'clock, but I had to return by 1 o'clock; we would get off at Babworth Bridge next to the main Eastern Region London-Edinburgh main line. First up was Class 'A3' No 60056 *Centenary*, then Class 'A1' No 60118 *Archibald Sturrock*, both incredibly shiny. I was hooked!

I then managed to get permission for all-day spotting, but still only at Retford. We would sit on the wall at the end of Platform 1 on a Saturday, and this was the highlight of my early days. To get a seat on the wall you had to get your bum on it by 9 o'clock otherwise you would be sitting on the platform surface – not good. We had the usual duffle bag packed with a bottle of pop, sauce sandwiches, Smiths crisps with the blue salt bag, and a black plastic 'pakamac'. The pakamac was the 'three-S' thing you put on when it was raining – sticky, stuffy and sweaty – and if you had rolled it up wet from the last time there was another 'S' – smelly. Very smelly. After finishing your grub you wandered off to the refreshment room to buy the same old things: a Lyons individual fruit pie and a Wagon Wheel, the Holy Grail of biscuits for kids at that time. I am sure you all remember how big they were, and look at them now, 50 years on – they are small, despite the fact that Burtons Biscuits say they are the same size now as they were in the 1950s and '60s, but then they were held by a much smaller hand. I am not convinced.

I quickly progressed to Doncaster, 18 miles away and the local Mecca – station, shed and the 'Plant' (the local name for the locomotive works). On a Saturday you could expect to see about 200 locos, and at least 14 'Streaks' ('A4s'); if it was your first day spotting you were off to a good start with the 'Streaks', as they were only a class of 34 locos.

The shed was relatively easy to get round without a permit. There were a couple of ways to negotiate your way past the foreman's office, but the golden rule was that once you were in (any shed) it was always best to get to the furthest point very quickly because if you got caught and ejected at least you had to walk back all the way through so you could get most of the numbers anyway.

The 'Plant' was a little more difficult. It was surrounded by a high wall at Hexthorpe Road, the main gate and paint shop end, a high wooden fence along the erecting shops, and a canal running the full extent of the other side. However, where there is a will there is a way. Just past the main gate at the end of a path that ran between the wooden perimeter fence and the backs of a row of houses you would find yourself at the south-east end of the 'Plant', where there was a small steel seven-bar gate that you could climb over. Once you were over

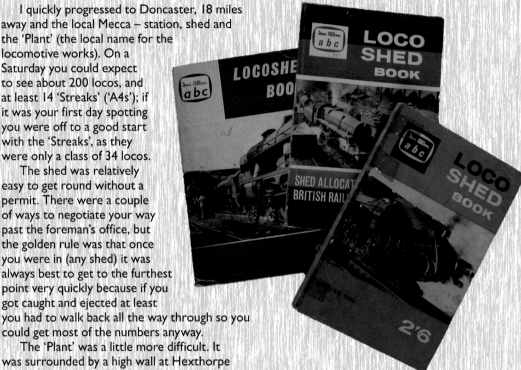

the fence you were in, and you were at the furthest point from the main entrance so it could only get better. If you went on a Sunday sometimes no one was working, so you could go where you wanted without being on the lookout for foremen and Transport Police. You just had to be careful when you got near the main security gate as its occupant might not be reading the paper!

My next goal was Crewe. This was reached via Sheffield and Manchester, and to get there on the cheap we would buy a cheap day return Worksop to Sheffield Victoria, then another Sheffield to Manchester Piccadilly, and one more Manchester to Crewe, all for under a pound. Later on I learned that if there was more than one of you, you could get from Worksop to Sheffield even cheaper. Only one of you would buy a cheap day return ticket and the others would just get on the train as Worksop was an open station. On arrival at Sheffield the one with the ticket would go through the barrier and buy platform tickets and bring them back to you so you could leave the station and buy the onward tickets. As the meerkats say these days, 'Simples!'

For Crewe I would leave Worksop just before 8 o'clock in the morning, arriving at 11.30am. En route you passed Darnall shed, went through Woodhead Tunnel, passed Gorton Works, Stockport Edgeley and Jodrell Bank before arriving at Crewe with four sheds and a works. What more could you ask for? The train back from Crewe would be about 5.30pm, so home at around 8.30pm.

Having said that, you still had to get round all the sheds, as this gave you many more numbers than just waiting on the station. My order of attack was first Crewe diesel depot, which was just outside the station, then work my way through on the right-hand side to Gresty Lane, the small GWR shed that only had about three locos, but it was like a magnet for me, just to see any Western Region engine. I probably did waste a lot of time looking at them, but it was on the way to Crewe South. For the South shed you just had to cross the main line

next to Gresty Lane and you were in, and on a good day you got 80 numbers.

Back over the line and through the diesel shed, I next attempted Crewe North – not an easy one. I only managed it once and even then only half of it. It was a straight shed with a roundhouse that was partially visible from the station, but not near enough to get the numbers. Then on to the works, which I would say were impossible to 'bunk', but on my first visit I was surprised to find that the British Transport Commission did daily guided tours round the works from the Eaton Street entrance at 2.00pm, costing just sixpence – what a good idea! All proceeds went to the Crewe Railway Charity Fund. Why didn't all the other sheds and works do this? It would have saved a lot of hassle!

Every step gets bigger, and next it had to be London. I was 13 and still only allowed to go to Retford or Doncaster. Crewe had been visited without Mam's permission, and London would certainly be the same. My plan was to do the quickest journey so I would have more time in the capital, and that meant going non-stop from Retford at 7.53am on the 'Master Cutler' Pullman, which was the normal price plus a 2s 9d each way Pullman supplement for under-14s. Yes, I was going to do it in style!

On my way back I had an evening meal. It was silver service and proper napkins. I ordered plaice and remember being asked by the waiter when it was served whether I would like tartare sauce; with no experience of restaurants, just local fish and chip shops, I thought he said

tomato sauce, so I promptly said, 'No thanks, I'll have brown.' I suppose he thought, 'Cheeky little git!'

You may wonder where a young lad got the money from in those days. Well, I was fortunate because may parents had a pub and they let me sell sweets from the off-licence – pubs don't have these nowadays. I use to order the sweets off a wholesaler from Mansfield called Clarvis, who use to deliver once a fortnight. I would sell them and keep the profit, which was about £3 per week – not bad money then. On occasions I would treat my mates who were not as lucky as me, and I would sometimes help them pay for their train tickets to wherever we were going.

When I first started spotting at Retford it was immediately noticeable that all the 'Pacifics' were always clean – virtually spotless, actually – and this added to the spectacle of seeing them speed past you at the lineside. It was only many years later that I found out why, being due to Peter Townend, who was shedmaster at King's Cross ('Top Shed') and took pride in his allocation, adopting this cleaning policy. Due to the small amount of railway publications in the late 1950s and '60s, this type of information was not commonly known amongst spotters; you just wonder what you could have done then if all of today's technology had been available to you – Internet, Google Maps, iPad, a car with sat-nav, digital cameras … the list is endless.

Another thing that did not really register was that when the 'A1s' were going past you did not appreciate that they were only just over ten years old, and you also did not know that they only had about five years' life left. It was an even worse situation with the 'Britannia' Class, some lasting just 14 years. I would look in *Trains Illustrated* to check what locos had been withdrawn, and it was usually about 100-odd a month, but I still did not realise that the end was getting nearer. I just thought it would go on for ever. Even when I saw lines of stored and withdrawn locos in the shed sidings I would just be glad to 'spot' them and search for more with no deep thought into the consequences of the locos being 'dead'.

It was one summer Sunday in 1959 that I went down the road to the lineside at Kilton, Worksop, and took the number 62660. It was not until about an hour later, when I got home and checked the numbers in the 'Combine', that it became apparent that it was actually a namer, *Butler-Henderson*. This amazed me as other spotters had said you only got 'namers' at Retford on the main line. It just shows how impressionable I was at that age, taking everything literally. I raced back down to the line and saw two more 'D11s', later discovering that they were being used most weekends on the seaside specials from Sheffield to the local East Coast resorts of Cleethorpes, Skegness and Bridlington.

On another occasion in 1958 a spotter who was in my class at St Augustine's junior school told me about the boat train that ran from Parkeston Quay to Manchester and Liverpool and passed through Worksop at about 12.15pm. From our upstairs classroom window we could just about see the top of any engine pass

through a gap in the trees, but could not get the number. He said that as he went home for dinner he could get the number for us. So all of us that stayed for school dinners and were not allowed outside the school gates went up to our classroom and waited and watched. Eventually it went past, and when the boy came back in the afternoon he said, 'Did you see it?' and when we said 'Yes' he said it was No 61633 *Kimbolton Castle*. Well, that was a cop for most of us, and the only 'B17' I ever saw. It was actually one of the last 'B17s' to haul the boat train, as the 'Britannias' then took over the duty. That was wonderful news for us, as very quickly we saw all the 22 'Brits' that were allocated to 32A Norwich Thorpe working the 'boaty'. We didn't have to watch them through the trees either, because we found out that the same loco was used for the return service that stopped at Worksop at 3.45pm, so as we finished school at 3.30pm we had plenty of time to see it at the station. This only lasted for about two years as progress meant that the new English Electric Type 3s took over, the 'Brits' being relocated to other regions.

In 1961 I managed to buy a Kodak 35mm camera. It was very basic with a set shutter speed of about 1/100th of a second and a couple of exposure settings – either cloudy, sun or very sunny – but I thought it was perfect. Well, after a couple of films with pictures mostly blurred and under- or over-exposed I realised its shortfalls. Having said that, when I look at the shots now some are quite reasonable given the camera's limitations. At the same time I started

developing and printing my own films with Paterson developing tanks and a Durst enlarger for the printing. I remember now loading films into the Paterson tank from the 35mm cassette under the bedclothes to block out every bit of light, otherwise it was a disaster. However, after loading a few you quickly became the expert.

It was a couple of years later in 1963 that I decided a better camera was needed. I had noticed that mature spotters were going around with Leica, Pentax and Rolleiflex cameras. Well, these were off the radar for me price-wise, so I went for a cheaper alternative, a German Exakta with a 2.8 Jena lens, and shutter speeds up to 1/1000th of a second, priced at £79. It had to be on hire purchase, with Mam as guarantor.

It was ordered from a camera shop in Sheffield, but the delay was about two weeks due to delivery and the approval of the hire purchase agreement. I actually collected it on 13 July 1963 and immediately started photographing any loco I saw. The camera did have another benefit in as much as prior to having it I 'bunked' most sheds, but when you had this good camera round your neck the foreman would look at you and think you looked sensible: 'Yes, you can go round, but be careful.' But we were *all* sensible. We didn't damage anything; we were mindful and careful. All we wanted to do was collect numbers and take photographs.

I started buying TriX film in long reels and loading my own cassettes. This worked out much cheaper; you could get up to 50 frames instead of the shop-bought 36. The only problem was that you did not know when you were winding on to the last frame – you had to just keep winding the film on till it stopped.

Fortunately I had the sense to keep all my negative strips in individual storage pockets, and after 55 years there is no evidence of any deterioration. It was in 2000 that I decided I would have a go at scanning all the negatives so I could view them on the computer. I did some research into what scanners were available and decided to buy a Scanace Prime Film 3600u, which was a dedicated 35mm scanner. Well, the instruction manual was written for a genius, not a beginner, so I had great difficulty in finding what the correct sequence was to produce a scan. I was a couple of days doing the same thing over and over again and getting the same result – nothing. I nearly took it back to the shop because it didn't work. Then I remembered a quote from a sales and marketing course I went on for work: 'If you always do what you have always done you will always get what you always got,' so I then experimented a little and on the third day I got a result with a scan that was not perfect, because it was a negative image and not positive, but it was progress. I couldn't find a way to make it positive with the scanner software, so I saved the file into a Microsoft photo program (can't remember the name) as I remembered seeing on the program's menu options the word 'Negative'. I opened up the photo file and selected 'Negative' and, bingo, it became positive – a perfect picture. This was the method I used for all my negatives. It was a slow process that took me a period of four years. Every time I scanned a negative and viewed it on the computer screen it was 'Wow!', and either a memory came flooding back or 'Crikey, that's good, did I take that?'

What you will notice from the photographs is the difference in the quality of the shots between the two cameras. The Kodak camera photos were 1961 to 1962 and are not as sharp, a little incorrect on exposure and, because it was not a single lens reflex, the shot might be a little off-centre. However, with the Exakta from 1963 onwards they are clearer, sharper, and a good exposure, and as it was an SLR what you saw in the pentaprism was what you got. Having said that, it is important to remember that all photographs are historically good, and 55 years later I could not recreate them – the subject matter has gone for ever.

Although I had some written records of what and where they were taken, it was largely incomplete so I started to make a comprehensive register using an Excel spreadsheet. It is surprising, though, when you see a photo how much information is still in your memory after all those years; I was at least able to make a start. Identifying the class and number was easy, and some of the locations were easy, but others needed the aid of the Internet to view other photos and images in order to recognise a place; sometimes simple things such as brickwork, telegraph poles and other buildings confirmed this. This took me about another four years, and now I have only 15 shots that I cannot confirm for certain where they were taken, but am still trying. After that my PC crashed and died; fortunately, I was backing up on CDs, so everything was safe, and it was at this point in 2008 that I decided to move to an Apple Mac and also to try and start a book.

How to tackle the book and what the theme should be took me some time to decide, but this is the result and I hope you enjoy my childhood memories!

1 • Worksop

'The Gateway to the Dukeries' – I can remember seeing the ornamental steel road signs as you entered Worksop from any direction, and I must confess it really did not mean anything to me as a lad; it was only when I was preparing this introduction that I found out what it meant. Apparently it was because south of the town there were four country houses and estates with Dukes in residence – Clumber House, Thoresby Hall, Welbeck Abbey and Worksop Manor – hence the term 'Dukeries'. The only one I ever visited as a young lad was Clumber Park on a couple of sunny Sunday afternoons on family outings; it must have been on the bus, as we did not have a car. I remember going through Lime Tree Avenue, which is the longest of its kind in Europe, being 2 miles long with 1,296 lime trees in two lines on either side of the road. Again, it did not register – if it had been two lines of steam locomotives that would have been different.

Arguably Worksop's most famous sports personality is golfer Lee Westwood, who became the world's number one in 2010, ending the reign of Tiger Woods; but probably close seconds are Mick Jones of Sheffield United and Leeds, and Graham 'Do I not like that' Taylor, the England manager.

The main employer after the Second World War was the National Coal Board, locally at Manton, Steetley and Shireoaks collieries, then a few more miles further out were the mines of Ollerton, Bevercotes, Thoresby and Welbeck. However, nothing lasts for ever and the decline of the industry started in the 1960s and escalated with the industrial actions of the 1970s and '80s, the industry now being non-existent.

Left: Everything starts here from my home town station of Worksop. This view shows an unidentified English Electric Type 3 with the Carlton Road level crossing gates closed, stopping the road vehicles, to allow it to go light towards Retford and let class 'O4/8' No 63612 through on a freight towards Sheffield, but more than likely branching off before then to one of the South Yorkshire pits.

Next to the 'O4/8' is the all-stations stopping train from Nottingham Midland, waiting in the sidings having shunted round the carriages to face the right way, but bunker-first for the return trip. It will also have been watered at one of the two water towers, one of which is on the left. It was mostly LMS 2-6-4 tanks on this duty, but occasionally it was one of Nottingham's Standard Class 2s. Further down the line you can just see two locos, both Class 'B1s'; they were stored in the sidings for about six months awaiting scrapping.

Notice the three boards of advertising posters on the left – I wonder what they would fetch at auction today… There is also a barrow-load of parcels that came off the Nottingham train, now waiting to be loaded again, probably to the Lincoln area. Closing the level crossing gates did cause traffic hold-ups even in the 1960s, when there were fewer cars, as the station was on the main road just north of the town centre. The worst time was when the Liverpool to Parkeston Quay boat train stopped in the afternoon about 4 o'clock; it had more coaches than the length of the platform, so had to move forward and stop again. Consequently the gates could be closed for 10 or more minutes – a time to be avoided. (26 July 1963)

Left: The Type 3 moves off and the 'O4/8', No 63612, comes through. On the right you can see the refreshment room where I spent many hours sipping pints (orange and water, nice and cheap) waiting for the next loco to come through. You never missed anything because when you heard the clanking of the gates opening it was time to go on to the platform. (26 July 1963)

Below left: The view looking in the opposite direction towards Sheffield sees an unidentified Class 'O2' on a coal train. On the right is the British Road Services depot, and next to the notice boards on the platform you can see my Carlton Catalina racing bike; these were locally made, and brilliant. (26 July 1963)

Below right: A couple of minutes earlier the same unidentified 'O2' entered Worksop station and passed the water tower at the end of Platform 1, which was for locomotives heading in the Sheffield direction. On the right is the partially covered wooden points shed, used for manually changing the points close by. As far as I remember it was only used for repositioning the coaches and locomotive of the Nottingham to Worksop service ready for the return journey. (26 July 1963)

Above: A large group of enthusiasts watch as Fairburn Class 4MT 2-6-4 tank No 42284 arrives from Nottingham Midland. They are actually waiting to bid farewell to the Worksop to Nottingham Midland service on Saturday 12 October 1964, as this was the final one due to cuts implemented under the Beeching plan. (12 October 1964)

Above rightt: Having been watered, shunted round the coaches and recoupled by Porter D. Hooley, No 42284 is ready to leave bunker-first with the last service to Nottingham Midland, the 8.07pm from Worksop, with driver Ken Wilcox of Nottingham in charge. A small group of well-wishers, letting off some fireworks on departure, had already daubed the train with 'Beeching Must Go' – just another piece of railway history now. Jim Reeves was in the pop charts with, appropriately, *I Won't Forget You*, and, as Max Boyce says, 'I was there.' (12 October 1964)

Rightt: Class 'K3/3' 2-6-0 No 61889 leaves Worksop for Sheffield Victoria with the 6.33pm train from Lincoln Central. Built in 1929 and eventually withdrawn on 4 November 1962, the engine was cut up at Cashmore's, Great Bridge. The 'B1s' then took over this duty. The 'K3s' were used for everything, passenger trains, fast fitted freights and fish trains, one of which came through Worksop every evening at about 7.00pm from one of the Humber ports. You could still smell the fish a long time after it had passed through, especially in the summer months. (1961)

This took us all by surprise. For about a month 'Royal Scot' Class No 46151 *The Royal Horse Guardsman* was solely in charge of the 6.33pm train from Lincoln Central to Sheffield Victoria, initially causing interest amongst the spotters, although it did wear off after a couple of weeks. It does demonstrate that in those days you never knew what locomotive was coming round the corner – that was the excitement of it all, the unpredictability! I did eventually work out what had happened; in 1960 she was allocated to 41C Millhouses operating on the Midland line from Sheffield either north to Leeds or south to Birmingham, but in mid-1962 she was relocated to 41A Darnall and was employed on the Sheffield to Lincoln route. It all ended at Darnall, the loco being withdrawn from there on 29 December 1962 after 32 years of service. (June 1962)

At 5.03pm English Electric Type 3 No D6744, with a very mixed assortment of freight wagons and, according to the headcode 'M', destined for the London Midland Region, is just approaching the signal box that was situated at the level crossing. (26 July 1963)

By 1963 English Electric Type 3s were hauling nearly all the passenger trains from Sheffield Victoria to destinations east, having taken over from the reliable 'B1s', and here is No D6746 in the Kilton area of Worksop with the 3.15pm Sheffield Victoria to Lincoln train. (10 August 1963)

With D6746 disappearing eastwards, another English Electric Type 3, No D6743, heads west with a Lincoln to Sheffield Victoria train passing Manton Colliery on the right. Worksop and the surrounding satellite council housing estates of Kilton and Manton were heavily populated mining communities. (10 August 1963)

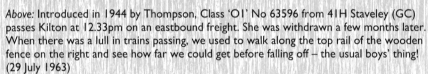

Above: Introduced in 1944 by Thompson, Class 'O1' No 63596 from 41H Staveley (GC) passes Kilton at 12.33pm on an eastbound freight. She was withdrawn a few months later. When there was a lull in trains passing, we used to walk along the top rail of the wooden fence on the right and see how far we could get before falling off – the usual boys' thing! (29 July 1963)

Above right: An unidentified English Electric Type 1, looking in ex-works condition, heading past Kilton towards Sheffield and presumably Tinsley depot. They were nearly always double-headed with a member of the same class and used on freight duties all year round, but on passenger duties only during the summer timetable, as they did not have any train heating facility for the winter months. (29 July 1963)

Right: Hauling the 'boat train' from Parkeston Quay to Liverpool and passing through Kilton at 12.19pm, virtually on time, is named English Electric Type 3; it is either No D6703 *The 1st East Anglia Regiment* or No D6707 *The 3rd East Anglia Regiment*. However, its nameplates are obscured by plywood covers due to an alleged dispute between British Railways and the Army, as the regiments had been amalgamated and the names were now inappropriate; they were removed two months later. (29 July 1963)

Retford 'O2' No 63964, one of our everyday regulars of the class, is running light in reverse at Kilton, maybe to the Worksop freight sidings to collect a coal train. (29 July 1963)

English Electric Type 3 No D6742 is seen at Kilton on the 3.45pm Sheffield Victoria to Lincoln service, with another train going in the opposite direction that includes in the rake a non-corridor coach with the recess for the destination headboard visible. If you look really closely you can see the pictures that were displayed in the compartments, standard attire in those days in non-corridor coaches. (29 July 1963)

An unidentified English Electric Type 3 with a rake of seven coaches approaches Worksop on another sunny day. All summer days seemed to be sunny when you were a lad – it never rained. Having said that, now I've retired I get the same feeling because when you were working the weather was good and weekends seemed to be bad; now I have seven days a week to enjoy and the vast majority of days seem good again. (29 July 1963)

Below: With Tinsley having an allocation of 36 English Electric Type 3s, they were now totally in control of both passenger and freight duties from the Sheffield area. This unidentified example is heading a Saturday seaside special to the Lincolnshire coast through Kilton. (10 August 1963)

Above: Relieving some of the boiler pressure, Class 'B1' No 61144 from 40B Immingham awaits the off for Retford and Lincoln with the usual rake of six coaches for those services. (1963)

2 • Retford

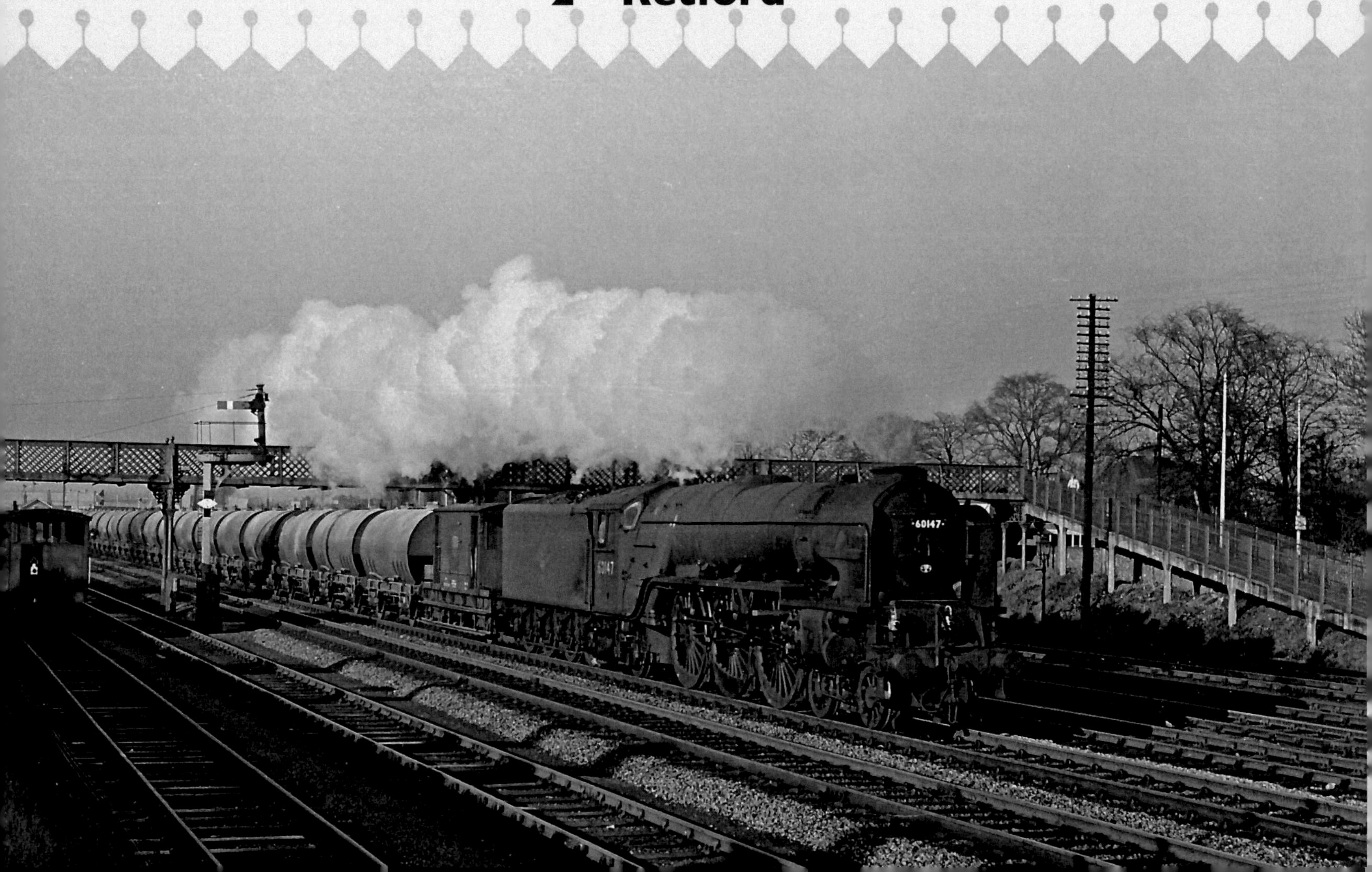

The North Nottinghamshire market town of Retford was dissected first by water, with the River Idle flowing north to south and the Chesterfield Canal east to west, then secondly from the mid-19th century by rail, with the East Coast Main Line running north to south and the Sheffield to Lincoln line going east to west. The railways helped promote industry in the area, mainly the brewery, paper mill, British Wire Ropes and the Northern Rubber Company, which was started by Alfred Pegler in 1871; years later his grandson, Alan Pegler, ran the company, and purchased Class 'A3' No 60103 *Flying Scotsman* from British Railways in 1963.

Retford had two loco sheds, both having the same code, 36E. Retford (GNR) was a four-track straight dead-end shed, while Retford (GCR) was a three-track straight shed with two through roads. The allocations were predominantly freight engines – 2-8-0s from Classes 'O1', 'O2' and 'O4' and a few 0-6-0 Class 'J6s' and 'J11s' – while local passenger duties were handled by the six or seven Class 'B1s' allocated there. The foremen of each shed were always accommodating to spotters and let you wander round, probably because the depots were small and activity was minimal, so it was relatively safe. Both sheds closed on the 14 June 1965.

It did not take very long for me to 'clear' (spot) all of Retford's allocation, so visits to the sheds became a low priority as there would be no 'cops', but this had regrettable consequences for my photo collection because when I did get a camera I only visited and took photos at the Great Northern shed. Oh, to be able to relive those days!

Left: Class 'A1' No 60147 *North Eastern* heads south on a sunny October afternoon in 1963. Only months earlier the 'Pacifics' had been employed on crack express passenger workings, but were now relegated to freight. No 60147 is only 14 years old and little does she know that there is only another year left before withdrawal in August 1964. (October 1963)

Right: North Eastern passes and approaches Whisker Hill Junction on the right and Retford station straight ahead, with the vast array of signalling in front and in the right distance. (October 1963)

Class 'B1' No 61212, one of the local workhorses employed on all duties, is just moving off with the Shell BP tanker and brake van, leaving the coal truck behind. You could virtually guarantee seeing her every day, either on Sheffield to Lincoln passenger trains or latterly freight duties. She was also a regular hauling the every-other-Saturday football special to Wadsley Bridge for Sheffield Wednesday home games, but is now, in October 1963, in a very run-down condition, but still hanging on for another year, being withdrawn on 1 November 1964. (October 1963)

An unidentified Class 'B1' with a local from Sheffield to Lincoln passes a spotter with a duffle bag, and another with an improvised wooden seat sitting in the middle of nowhere – probably the wall was full. Five more are hanging round the cab trying to pluck up enough courage to ask 'Can we cab it?' Fashions had just started to change, and with the brown duffle coat are now long trousers rather than short. (April 1961)

An unidentified 'Britannia' 'Pacific' on the Liverpool to Parkeston Quay 'boat train' crosses the East Coast Main Line at right angles. All the spotters standing at the end of Platform 1 as it speeds through get a good view; the one on the end in school uniform with his satchel has just finished his day at Retford Grammar School. (April 1961)

Right: Prototype Brush Type 4 No D0280 *Falcon* on the Sheffield to King's Cross afternoon Pullman, with its rake of slab-sided and Metro-Cammell cars, negotiates Whisker Hill curve, passing on the right the Worksop & Retford Brewery Company. It was such a tight radius that you could hear all the wheels grinding and screeching as trains rounded the curve at the imposed 10 miles per hour maximum speed limit. The morning Sheffield Victoria to King's Cross and evening return expresses were called the 'Master Cutler' – 'I'll have brown, please…' (1963)

Left: Class 'A4' No 60021 *Wild Swan* departs for King's Cross, but has been diverted onto the Lincoln line because of track maintenance south of Retford, probably adding an hour to the total journey. She was in her final year, withdrawal coming on 20 October 1963. (September 1962)

Above: 'A1' No 60138 *Boswell* departs for Doncaster with an afternoon stopping train from King's Cross to York. It is the autumn of 1961, and luckily she hung on to the end, being withdrawn some four years later – a good effort. Just visible blending in with the smokebox door is the 10 miles per hour maximum speed sign for the branch line to Worksop around the Whisker Hill curve. (1961)

Above right: In the afternoon sun at the Great Northern shed, 36E Retford, Class 'B1' No 61127 waits for the next duty from her home shed; this was another local hard-working see-it-every-day 'B1' still in very good condition. In all, 410 'B1s' were built, making them one of the largest classes, but Edward Thompson made a controversial decision by placing building orders with independent companies, 290 with the North British Locomotive Company and 50 with Vulcan Foundry, rather than the traditional railway works. (October 1963)

Right: Having just passed the cattle market on the line from Worksop, Class 'O4' No 63661 is waiting for the 'all clear' to proceed and cross the East Coast Main Line, which from this approach was at right angles. (October 1963)

Above: From Robinson's original design with cab side windows, Class 'O4' No 63726 lies idle in the shed but with a tender full of coal waiting for the next duty. Note the slightly bent frame near the front, presumably from heavy-handed shunting – this was a common sight on this class. (October 1963)

Above right: Class 'A1' No 60134 *Foxhunter*, trapped by wagons, languishes in the shed. She remained there for about two months after failing on an express; she was, however, repaired and continued in service until 4 October 1965. (1961)

Righte: Probably formerly an 'A4' duty, now the 'Deltics' have arrived, this one named but unidentifiable with what appears to be an incredible 18-coach train, having gone through the 'double peg' London signal. On the left is the now rarely used platform water crane. (October 1963)

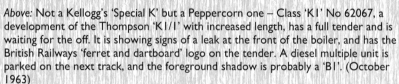

Above: Not a Kellogg's 'Special K' but a Peppercorn one – Class 'K1' No 62067, a development of the Thompson 'K1/1' with increased length, has a full tender and is waiting for the off. It is showing signs of a leak at the front of the boiler, and has the British Railways 'ferret and dartboard' logo on the tender. A diesel multiple unit is parked on the next track, and the foreground shadow is probably a 'B1'. (October 1963)

Above right: Class 'B1' No 61055 simmers in the afternoon sun on the approach roads to the GN shed, her home. (October 1963)

Right: 'B1' No 61225 is also at her home shed, and underneath the shed plate is the 'SC' plate, denoting 'Self Cleaning'; this was a wire-mesh device fitted inside the smokebox that caused most of the char drawn through the boiler tubes to be thrown out of the chimney, rather than collecting in the smokebox. (October 1963)

Below: A development of the experimental Gresley GNR three-cylinder locomotive, Class 'O2' No 63975 is in perfect running condition and parked up for the weekend waiting to start freight duties again on Monday, more than likely movement of coal from one of the many South Yorkshire and North Nottinghamshire pits. (October 1963)

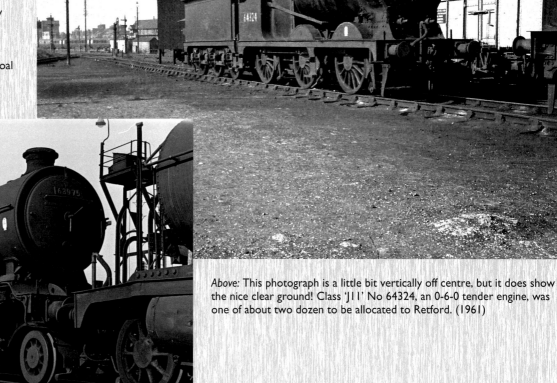

Above: This photograph is a little bit vertically off centre, but it does show the nice clear ground! Class 'J11' No 64324, an 0-6-0 tender engine, was one of about two dozen to be allocated to Retford. (1961)

Above: Waiting outside the GN shed, which was a brick-built dead-end four-track straight shed, is original Robinson 'O4/1' No 63727, built in 1911 with a small boiler, Belpaire firebox, steam and vacuum brakes and water scoop. 'B1' No 61127 is at its side for a bit of company in the sunshine. The shed closed in 1965. (October 1963)

Above right: This view shows three of the four roads of the GN shed, with 'B1s' Nos 61213 and 61126, and 'O4' No 63688. (1961)

Right: This 'J94' saddle tank is one of the two allocated to the shed, either No 68067 or No 68075. What a nice corrugated steel shed with a pile of wood for the stove and brazier next to it! (1961)

A 'Deltic' approaches from the north for King's Cross, speeding down the 1 in 440 gradient having got the all clear with the 'double peg' on the semaphores. (October 1963)

'Deltic' No D9010, then unnamed but eventually becoming *The King's Own Scottish Borderer* in May 1965, hauls the down 'Queen of Scots' Pullman from King's Cross to Edinburgh and Glasgow, sporting the '1S57' train identification number. The first car is an original 'slab-sided', while the rest are the new Metro-Cammell vehicles. Its route was not the normal East Coast Main Line, but branched off at Doncaster and went via Leeds and Harrogate before rejoining at Northallerton; the journey time to Glasgow was 8hr 40min. Here you see it crossing the intersection of the Great Northern and Great Central lines and passing Retford South signal box. (October 1963)

Above: It is getting near dusk and a slight mist is coming in on an October evening as 9F No 90590, from 41F Mexborough, after waiting a good 10 minutes on the opposite side of the crossing, is given the all clear and crosses over the GN line with a freight from the Worksop direction. (October 1963)

Above right: 'A3' No 60049 *Galtee More* was the first of the class to be fitted with German-type smoke deflectors as a result of recommendations from Peter Townend, the shedmaster at King's Cross. Some were actually fitted on shed and not when in for a service at either Doncaster or Darlington works. As you can see the appearance caused a lot of interest in the early days if you had not seen this type of deflector before; eventually 55 of the class of 79 were fitted with them from 1961 onwards. (1961)

Right: English Electric Type 4 No D272 pulls away from Platform 1 heading towards London in the afternoon and displaying a Class 1 headcode for an express. The second man has his window down, feeling the heat of the sun and the diesel engines, while two spotters, one in long and one in short trousers, look on. The Type 4s were once the pride of the diesel fleet, the majority being built at the Vulcan Foundry, Newton-Le-Willows; 200 were built, and they operated on the Eastern, London Midland and Scottish regions. (October 1963)

'Deltic' No D9012 *Crepello* heads an express from King's Cross to Edinburgh. Note the lineside telegraph poles and telegraph wires in abundance, and the 'somersault' signal on the right for the road to the GN shed sidings. (October 1963)

'Deltic' No D9002 *The King's Own Yorkshire Light Infantry* heads an up passenger train. For a short time this loco shared a similar name with Class 'V2' No 60872, which was *King's Own Yorkshire Light Infantry*, with no 'The'. (October 1963)

Brush Type 4 No D1507 arrives at Retford 7 minutes late with the 7.50am train from Leeds Central to King's Cross, with Whisker Hill curve going off to the left to connect with the line to Worksop and Sheffield. (20 July 1963)

It was most unusual to see a diesel locomotive at the Retford sheds, but here is Brush Type 2 No D5689 off 41A Sheffield Darnall, which has probably failed locally and is awaiting attention. (September 1962)

3 • Doncaster

Doncaster, or 'Donny' as it is known locally, is another market town and was in the centre of the South Yorkshire coalfields with easy transportation links by water, road and rail by the River Don, the A1 and the East Coast Main Line respectively. Thus its locomotive allocation was mainly freight for the transportation of coal for export and coal for the steel mills of Sheffield, Rotherham and Scunthorpe. It has a racecourse, and probably the most famous event is the St Leger Stakes, the world's oldest classic, which started in 1776 and is held every September; if you look through the list of winners you will find that most of the Gresley 'A3s' are named after them.

For railway enthusiasts, however, it was known for the locomotive works and Stirling's 8-foot 'Singles', Ivatt's 'Atlantics' and the Gresley, Thompson and Peppercorn 'Pacifics'. The 'Plant' was a big employer in the Doncaster area, in 1962 providing work for around 3,600 people in the locomotive and carriage works combined.

Another railway connection is Doncaster Grammar School (now Hall Cross Academy), founded in 1350. In the early 1930s the pupils and teachers founded a railway society, and since then they have been collecting railway memorabilia, amassing about 2,000 items; viewing is by appointment but well worth a look.

This is one of the 720 Austerity 2-8-0 locomotives that Riddles designed for the Ministry of Supply; they were employed in large numbers around the coalfield areas and were distinctive for the noise they produced, a dull clanking sound. Here is No 90252, with steam being emitted from all quarters, at the head of an iron-ore train bound for the Sheffield/Rotherham area. (11 August 1963)

It is just four days after the 'Great Train Robbery', and the time is 4.20 according to the 'Plant' clock on this Sunday afternoon. The view is from St James's Bridge looking north towards the station. On the right is the British Railways parcels depot, and Class 'A1' No 60149 *Amadis* is on station pilot duty. An English Electric Type 3 is in the station, then on the left is a Brush Type 4, a Brush Type 2, rows of withdrawn coaches, and four Class 'J50s' that were primarily used on shunting duties in and around the 'Plant'. Just to the right of the 'J50s' is the Plant Weigh House; when No 60103 (4472) *Flying Scotsman* was purchased from British Railways by Alan Pegler it was housed there for a period.

Crossing the station is the pedestrian overbridge that started in the station approach and went straight into the 'Plant' through the engineering offices on the left, for the convenience of the workers. I often thought about trying to 'bunk' the 'Plant' via this entry, but just could not pluck up enough courage, so I went my usual way along Hexthorpe Road to the main gate entrance to seek permission; if it was not granted, which was usual, I would walk another quarter of a mile and climb the gate.

Before Health & Safety, in the foreground you can see nine British Railways staff checking the track, although it looks more to me as double time on Sunday and they are having a break! Perhaps one of them in the centre group is having his 40-year trade union membership service award presentation – is this his badge? This picture might have inspired Ray and Dave Davies of the Kinks to write *Sunny Afternoon* some three years later... (11 August 1963)

Above: English Electric Type 4 No D252, displaying an express passenger headcode, is due to leave Doncaster for the north. They were a class of 200, and 25 of them operating on the London Midland Region were named after ships of the Cunard, Elder Dempster and Canadian Pacific lines. The most infamous of the class was No D326, which hauled the Glasgow to London Euston mail train that was the subject of the 'Great Train Robbery'. (1961)

Above right: Class 'A3' No 60103 *Flying Scotsman*, nice and clean off 34A Kings Cross, is seen here in virtually its original form, and as I remember them best, with double chimney and before being fitted with the German-type smoke deflectors. She is awaiting departure from Platform 8 with a semi-fast train from London to Newcastle; the young boy seems more interested in what is pulling the goods train! (1961)

Right: In a different guise as preserved No 4472, *Flying Scotsman* runs light from the sheds to the station to take over the Gresley Society's 'London North Eastern Flyer' from sister engine No 60106 *Flying Fox*, which brought in the special from King's Cross. (2 May 1964)

Flying Fox arrives with the Gresley Society's nine-coach special. According to timings it attained 95 mph on the descent of Stoke bank during the return journey.

No 60106 was credited with 2,642,860 miles over her 41-year career, thought to be the highest mileage of any British steam locomotive. (2 May 1964)

Above: Flying Scotsman leaves Doncaster for Darlington with the 'London North Eastern Flyer' special, which ran from King's Cross to Darlington and return together with a visit to Darlington Works. In the background, left to right, are a diesel shunter, an English Electric Type 3, a Brush Type 4, a Brush Type 2 and a multiple unit. (2 May 1964)

Above right: An unidentified English Electric Type 5 'Deltic' hauls the 1.00pm train from King's Cross to Newcastle with a rake of 13 coaches. After stopping for a signal check it is passing the carriage sidings that are just adjacent to the spur to the Sheffield line. The plume of exhaust from the 'Deltic' shows that it is accelerating after the hold-up, but not for long as it has a scheduled stop at Doncaster. (11 August 1963)

Right: Heading the 1.52pm Sunderland to King's Cross train, English Electric Type 4 No D355 leaves Doncaster and passes under St James's Bridge with four adult spotters looking over and the spire of the church of St James beyond. If you were a small boy you would have no chance of seeing anything from the bridge, but it was a popular gathering point, although I much preferred being on the station and sitting on a trolley. (11 August 1963)

Below: Class 'A1' No 60156 *Great Central* has nameplates with hand-painted crests. There are not many passengers about, just a few spotters all apparently uninterested in the local Doncaster 'A1' at Platform 4, which was my favourite vantage point on the station. (1961)

Above: Shunter No D4079, later Class 08, performs duties with a small three-plank open goods wagon, passing the breakers' yard that is full of military tanks for scrap; maybe if they had been saved there would not be the alleged shortfall of equipment now...? (1961)

Below: Gresley 'K3/2' 2-6-0 No 61946 arrives at Platform 1 with a stopping train from Hull – confirmed by the headcode. Just a couple of months earlier this was a duty for a 'D49' 'Hunt' Class engine. No 61946 was actually based at 31B March, so was presumably making her way back there and not taking the train back to Hull; she was withdrawn in June 1962. (1961)

Above: Class 'A3' No 60108 *Gay Crusader* stands by the relatively new electric signal gantry, its train being loaded with a trolley full of parcels. On the right a group of boys are walking across the 'Plant' overbridge – obviously they had permits to go round the works. (1961)

Brush Type 4 No D1504 approaches Doncaster station for a scheduled stop with the 12.20pm from King's Cross to Leeds Central. In the distance you can see a bridge over the railway; if you were going to attempt the sheds you would walk up St Sepulchres Gate, and turn and left just before you reached that bridge into St Swithin Terrace, continue into Kellam Street, then a right turn into Oak Terrace and you were at the sheds. (11 August 1963)

'Deltic' No D9000 *Royal Scots Grey* leaves Doncaster with the Sunday 1A35 10.50am service from Edinburgh Waverley for King's Cross stopping at Newcastle, York, Doncaster, Grantham and Peterborough, a total journey time of 7hr 29min.

On weekdays and Saturdays 1A35 was the 'Flying Scotsman' service, which only stopped at Newcastle with a journey time of 6 hours. (11 August 1963)

4 • Doncaster 'Plant'

You can see my unofficial entrance to the 'Plant' – the seven-bar tubular steel gate – on the right of Brush Type 2 No D5604, in original livery. In the USA Billboard pop charts at No 3 that week was one-hit-wonder Doris Troy with *Just One*

Look, and that's all we spotters wanted. It was actually a UK hit later in 1964 and reached No 2 sung by my namesake in the Hollies. (21 July 1963)

Above: Another Brush Type 2, No D5655, is seen outside the bottom end of the Crimpsall erecting shops. These diesels were used extensively on local passenger trains, and those based at 41A Sheffield Darnall replaced the Class 'B1' and 'D11' locomotives on their workings, particularly on the summer weekend seaside excursion specials, only to be later replaced themselves by the English Electric Type 3s. (17 August 1962)

Above right: 'A4' No 60009 *Union of South Africa* survived the cutter's torch – not much to see, but if you needed it, it was a 'cop'. I couldn't see anything else from the 'Union', only the tender behind it, which could have been hers. She was eventually outshopped – with corridor tender No 5332 and refurbished boiler No 29337 – having taken 114 days for a General service. (21 July 1963)

Right: We're now inside the famous Crimpsall erecting shop with its huge glass roof. It's 4 o'clock on a Sunday – nobody about, just the quiet of dead locomotives in their hospital. Class 'A4' No 60029 *Woodcock* is midway through her 31-day Light Casual Repair, but was withdrawn some three months later. (21 July 1963)

Class 'B1' 4-6-0 No 61406 is all stripped down for a General service and the fitting of 100A boiler No 28269.
In the next chapter you will see her some three weeks later, immaculately turned out. (21 July 1963)

Left: About a year earlier in the Crimpsall, Brush Type 2 No D5542 and a couple of British Railways/BTH Type 2s are all receiving attention. It's very labour-intensive, with what looks like a young apprentice on the left and the two in flat caps looking like twins. You just wonder who they all are — obviously the older men will have progressed from steam to diesel. (17 August 1962)

Right: Into the steam bays for a famous 'racehorse', the unbeaten Triple Crown-winner *Ormonde* in the guise of Class 'A3' No 60057 in for a General. The young fitter is hiding his cup of tea behind his back, looking to see if the foreman is about — maybe it's not break time yet... (17 August 1962)

Left: Now in the open yards we see ex-British Railways Class 'J50' No 68917, but now Departmental locomotive No 12, used mainly on duties associated with the 'Plant'.
In the film *The Great St Trinian's Train Robbery* two Class 'J94' locomotives were used, but so the audience did not get confused one of them was made to look like a 'J50' by having false extended side tanks fitted and being numbered 68961. I remember going to the Coliseum cinema in Newport to see the film in 1966 and watching it for an hour and a half standing at the back upstairs because it was full! (21 July 1963)

Right: Class 'A1' No 60162 *Saint Johnstoun*, always a Scottish engine, was down for servicing, but it did not last much longer, being officially withdrawn on 28 October 1963 and apparently being cut up in another loco hospital, Inverurie Works, in February 1964. (21 July 1963)

Class 'A3' 'Pacific' No 60090 *Grand Parade* is coupled to a Great Northern Railway coal-rail tender.
She managed to leave the 'Plant' but remained in service only until the end of October,
being cut up at Cowlairs Works on 24 January 1964. (21 July 1963)

Above: Class 'N2' No 69523 was built with a small chimney to suit workings at Moorgate, London, over lines governed by the Metropolitan Line loading gauge; it has also been fitted with condensing apparatus. It was purchased for preservation in September 1963 by the Gresley Society and is now based on the Great Central Railway at Loughborough in GNR livery running as No 1744. (21 July 1963)

Above right: The majority of locomotives in the 'Plant' were 'Pacifics', and quite a few were what for us were the rarer Scottish engines, much to our delight. Here is Class 'A3' No 60094 *Colorado*, one of those from across the border – Haymarket – down for treatment and even before her overall looking in very good condition, dressed with everything except the shed code plate – had someone managed to get this off? (21 July 1963)

Right: The famous first 'A4', No 60014 *Silver Link*, was in the 'Plant' for about a year waiting for a decision on preservation, the interested party being Sir Billy Butlin, but it was not to be – what a missed opportunity. I saw her a few times in the works during that period and I have always wondered whether I should have tried to get the nameplate or the works plate off her. I think somebody got one of the works plates because Christies sold one in their Railway Art and Literature sale of 21 July 1988, lot number 142, with a guide price of £1,000-£2,000. It sold for £8,000. The story goes someone found it in a cellar together with the works plate off *Quicksilver* (also in the sale as lot number 143) – can you believe it? (21 July 1963)

Above: 'A4' No 60008 *Dwight D. Eisenhower* had been officially withdrawn the day before I saw her, but she was lucky, and was reprieved and shipped to the National Railroad Museum, Green Bay, Wisconsin, USA, for preservation. After her brief repatriation in 2013 for the 'Great Gathering' of 'A4s' at the National Railway Museum, York, she is now back in the USA – here's hoping they keep her in better condition this time! (21 July 1963)

Above right: Parked in front of 'A2' 'Pacific' No 60526 *Sugar Palm* is 'A4' No 60006 *Sir Ralph Wedgwood* in a very clean condition prior to having her service – maybe as a result of the enthusiasm of the legendary shedmaster at King's Cross 'Top Shed', Peter Townend, who kept his 'Pacifics' spotlessly clean. (October 1962)

Right: 'A4' No 60013 *Dominion of New Zealand* was one of five of the class to be named after British Empire countries. She looks as though she is receiving some attention to her whistle while in for a 39-day Light Casual. (March 1962)

Above: Records are there to be broken, and LNER locomotive 'A4' No 2509 *Silver Link* held the world speed record for steam at 112.5mph, but then No 2512 *Silver Fox* reached 113mph. In 1937 the record went to the LMS with No 6220 *Coronation* achieving 114mph, but then on 3 July 1938 'A4' No 60022 *Mallard* smashed the lot of them with 126mph. Here she is in the 'Plant' having a Light Casual, which took 25 days. She is missing the commemorative plaque confirming that 126mph had been achieved, still a record for a steam locomotive; the plaque was probably locked away in the 'Plant' safe. (March 1962)

Above:right 'A4' No 60031 *Golden Plover* was another class member named after a bird, as Nigel Gresley was a keen bird-watcher. Brush Type 2 No D5814 is also in for 25 days, but according to records it was an unclassified repair. (March 1962)

Right: Class 'A2' No 60526 *Sugar Palm* off 50A York is also in for a check, but was soon to be condemned, still complete with the railway collectables – name, number, shed and makers plates – all to be sold at 1962 giveaway prices, but even then I still could not afford them. Note the use of wooden rather than metal ladders. (October 1962)

Above: 'A2' No 60517 *Ocean Swell*, a long-wheelbase variant, was based at North East depots, but never moved again, being withdrawn in November 1962 and cut up at the 'Plant'. (17 August 1962)

Right: This is where they ended up: a boiler is strung up on the Carruthers overhead gantry crane. I always checked this area for number, name and works plates – no such luck for me, but I bet some others were lucky. (17 August 1962)

Above: This rear view of the cab of Class 'A2' 'Pacific' No 60121 *Silurian*, parked in front of the boiler testing shop next to the traverser, makes you realise the crude cramped conditions that drivers and firemen worked in, shovelling coal and being tossed from side to side at say 70 to 80 miles an hour for 6 hours – not the glamour job I would have liked daily. (21 July 1963)

Left: Class 'A4' 4-6-2 No 60010 *Dominion of Canada* is at the start of its routine overhaul schedule. It survived in service until 29 May 1965, and fortunately was preserved; it is now on static display in the Canadian Railway Museum, Montreal. You can just see another 'A4' by the chimney on the left. (April 1963)

Right: Delivered new from English Electric Robert Stephenson & Hawthorn Ltd, Darlington, are two English Electric Type 3s, Nos D6823 and D6822, with Brush Type 4 No D1508, not so new, alongside. The Type 3s are going through initial acceptance inspections, then they were usually used on a couple of passenger trains to Sheffield Victoria for live testing before entering normal service, when they were both allocated to 88A Canton. (April 1963)

5 • Doncaster 36A

Class 'O1' No 63594 is 'dead' in the yard, with the 'Cenotaph' automated coaling and sanding stage about seven tracks behind it. Just visible tucked in behind the tender is one of the 'new breed', a Brush Type 4. (11 August 1963)

Left: Class 'O4/8' No 63836, with no coupling rods and only the shell of the cylinder casing, is presumably awaiting transfer to the 'Plant' to face the cutter's torch. If someone lit her fire it would just be like the 1963 Peter, Paul and Mary hit *Blowing In The Wind.* (11 August 1963)

Right: In this track-level view, Class 'B1' No 61104 is minus its shed plate, but was a 41D Canklow engine. It looks as though it is on some sort of scrap line, but it isn't – it's got another eight months of operating out of Canklow. (11 August 1963)

A remarkably clean but not ex-works Class 'A1' No 60128 *Bongrace* poses in what is photogenically considered the best position for the motion and coupling rods. It is on its home shed with a year and a half left, being withdrawn on 10 January 1965. Doncaster at this time had an allocation of 13 A1s', and from memory all were kept in a clean condition. (11 August 1963)

Left: This is Class 'A3' No 60063 *Isinglass*, with double chimney and German-type smoke deflectors. Most of the 'A3s' were named after racehorses and this was one of them; for you racing men, at the age of three Isinglass won the 2,000 Guineas, the Epsom Derby and, locally on the Doncaster track, the St Leger Stakes. He only lost one race in his career, finishing second in the Lancashire Plate, and in all his races he had just the one jockey, Tommy Loates. So remember that for the pub quiz! (11 August 1963)

Below: After overnight rain, 'A1' No 60138 *Boswell* stands trapped by an 'O4' and a 'WD' just in front of the brick-built 12-road straight-through shed. She was Darlington-built with a non-riveted tender, and was one of 13 'A1s' that were also named after racehorses, Boswell having been the St Leger winner in 1936. (11 August 1963)

Right: Once a local freight workhorse, although not one of Doncaster's, Class 'O4' No 63645's final depot was 41J Langwith Junction, and prior to that only 10 miles away at 41F Mexborough. But she's now dead in the sidings with no evidence of coal in the tender, and will be withdrawn on 14 April 1964 after a working life of 46 years, during which she was serviced at Gorton Works 20 times, and will be scrapped by W. E. Smith's of Ecclesfield. (11 August 1963)

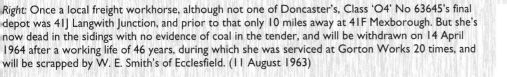

Left: Class 9F 2-10-0 No 92179 is ready for the off as the driver climbs aboard, most likely going on a duty back home as the engine wasn't local but was from New England, Peterborough. Doncaster only had an allocation of ten 9Fs working to the coalfields or steelworks at Scunthorpe, but they always had a large presence on shed due to 'foreign' arrivals. (11 August 1963)

Right: I bet this could be the end for Class 'B1' No 61080 after bumping someone's rear at a roundabout, with the usual 50/50 blame on the insurance! (11 August 1963)

Above: Doncaster Class 'B1' No 61196 is waiting in steam at the southern end of the shed, with the tender of another 'B1', No 61080, in front. She was withdrawn on 4 July 1964 but reinstated some 17 days later, the final call coming on 26 September 1965; two months later she was sold for scrap to T. W. Ward, Beighton. (11 August 1963)

Right: A pair of near identical twins, Class 'A1' Nos 60125 *Scottish Union* and 60114 *W. P. Allen*, are positioned on 11 and 12 roads respectively, next to the lifting shop on the right. They are both at their home shed, probably having returned after a late night out, and are doing what Frank Ifield was singing about, *Confessin'*, which was No 1 in the charts at the time! (11 August 1963)

Below: Now that's more like it! Class 'B1' No 61406 is in her Sunday best having been outshopped from the 'Plant' two days earlier after a General overhaul and repaint – it's a pity the fitters forgot to disconnect the table lamp from the dome! She is surrounded by five 'WDs', a 9F and what looks like the rear of an 'A3' with a GN tender. The foreman's office, with the veranda, can be seen through the gap in the locos; this was the only time I did the shed with an official permit – I must have had a mental blockage! (11 August 1963)

Above: The last time York Peppercorn Class 'K1' 2-6-0 No 62063 had a service was November 1962, and she is now looking like a lick of paint would do her good – but it was not to be, and she was withdrawn in September 1964. (11 August 1963)

Left: This is Doncaster's Class 'K1' 2-6-0 No 62066. A total of 70 were built by the North British Locomotive Company, Glasgow, in 1949, and the last of the class remained in service until December 1967. One, No 62005, was preserved and can now be seen operating on the West Highland Line. (11 August 1963)

Below left: Only at Doncaster for a couple of months, then transferred to New England before withdrawal in October 1964, Class 'A3' No 60112 *St Simon* is in steam with a GN-type tender in the company of English Electric Type 4 No D356, carrying a 50A York shed plate, and 9F 2-10-0 No 92181, also in steam. *St Simon* was originally built in 1923 as a Class 'A1', but was rebuilt to 'A3' specification in 1946. (11 August 1963)

Below: The 'V2' Class were mainly employed on freight duties, although categorised as mixed-traffic locomotives. They had the distinction of being the only major 2-6-2 tender engine used in Britain. A total of 184 were built at Doncaster and Darlington between 1936 and 1944, but they took a big hit in 1962/63 when 112 were withdrawn. This example, No 60924, survived until 22 September 1963 and was scrapped at Doncaster Works on 5 November of that year. (11 August 1963)

Left: At the northern end of the shed, with the usual damaged front running plate, is Class 'O4' 2-8-0 No 63593, surrounded by two 'heavies', 9F 2-10-0s. (11 August 1963)

Below left: Already withdrawn some eight months earlier, Class 'O2' 2-8-0 No 63971, latterly a Retford engine, will not be here for much longer, being scrapped by Central Wagon Co, Wigan, in September 1963. (11 August 1963)

Below: Class 'WD' No 90002 is in ex-works condition, and it was not very often that you would see them in this condition. They were usually grimy, oil- and water-stained – a typical heavy-duty freight engine, just like the LMS Class 8F on which the 'WD' design was based. (11 August 1963)

Gay Crusader, an English Triple Crown-winner in 1917, ran a total of ten races, winning eight, all at Newmarket because of wartime restrictions. No 60108, seen here, was named after it, but is not in steam, lacks a shed code and probably didn't have another duty as she was withdrawn in October and cut up at Darlington in November 1963. (11 August 1963)

Above: With 'V2' No 60974 to the right and 'A3' No 60065 *Knight of Thistle* to the left, Class 'O4/8' No 63801 is a Robinson-designed 2-8-0 built in 1918 as a Class 'O4/3'. It was requisitioned by the War Department Railway Operating Division (ROD) for service in Europe during the First World War. As an 'O4/3' she was built with steam brakes only and no water scoop, then in May 1956 she entered Gorton Works for a General overhaul and at the same time was fitted with a type 100A (Class 'B1') boiler and reclassified as 'O4/8'. (11 August 1963)

Right: Standing next to a timber five-plank open goods wagon, Class 'O1' 2-8-0 No 63678 seems to be sporting a digital television aerial 40 years ahead of it's time – nobody else had one in Doncaster! (11 August 1963)

Below: It's not surprising that in a heavily populated mining area Class 'WDs' would have a large presence on shed. No 90569, in typically grimy condition and looking like the dirt is holding it in one piece, is motionless so not clanking. (11 August 1963)

Above: An imposing ground-level view of War Department 8F No 90018. A total of 935 were built to a design adapted from the LMS 8F by Riddles for the Ministry of Supply. They were a much simplified construction with many interchangeable parts and a steel firebox, thus achieving low cost rather than long design life. For the war effort they served in mainland Europe, and after the war 184 stayed there, working mostly in the Netherlands, and 12 were exported to Hong Kong to work on the Kowloon-Canton Railway. (11 August 1963)

Above: Class 'A4' 'Pacific' No 60032 *Gannet* is not as green as a Top Shed turn-out, but is in store just before its official withdrawal notice came through on 20 October 1963. She was cut up at Doncaster some six weeks later. (11 August 1963)

Above: No 63741, originally a ROD 2-8-0 but now a Class 'O4/8', is carrying on for another two years before the end. (11 August 1963)

Left: Hello, hello, hello – what have we here? A foreigner, a '4er'. If you only had an Ian Allan Eastern Region 2s 6d book, you could not underline this – you would need the London Midland Region version or a *Combined Volume.* Ivatt 4MT 2-6-0 No 43105 is one of the original single-chimney versions. (11 August 1963)

Right: Class 'A1' No 60138 *Boswell* was from 50A York and, like *Bongrace* seen earlier, looks remarkably clean, particularly as the 'Pacifics' were in a period of decline and being relegated to secondary mundane duties rather than the express passenger services for which they were built. (11 August 1963)

Class 'A4' No 60010 *Dominion of Canada* leaves the 'Cenotaph' having just been coaled. The spotter walking across the eight or nine tracks of the shed yards to get a closer view of the 'Streak' is dressed in a belted gabardine mac, short trousers, long socks, probably with elastic bands holding them up, and his school satchel. I can remember when I developed this photograph looking at it and wondering why I had taken it with the boy in the way – well, 50 years on I am glad I did, for the candid shot and the nostalgia. (1961)

6 • Journey to Crewe

From 1946 until 2002 Crewe was the home of Rolls-Royce car production, and since then the Pyms Lane factory has produced the Bentley motor car. But really Crewe is known as a railway centre, with six lines converging from Chester, Glasgow, Manchester, Derby, London and Shrewsbury, and the home of railway workshops. Just after the Second World War the works employed about 8,500 people, and by the end of steam it had built more than 7,000 locomotives, notably the Stanier 'Princess Coronation' Class and the majority of the 'Jubilee' and 'Black Five' classes. Due to all this it was yet another Mecca for trainspotters; if you managed to get round all the sheds and the works and spent a few hours on the station you could expect to see more than 400 locos.

Crewe also has a football club nicknamed The Railwaymen because of the town's links with the railway industry. The club is famous for the pub quiz question: 'Name five of the original 92 Football League teams that have an "x" in their name.' Crewe was usually the one people failed to get because they remember Crewe and not Crewe Alexandra. I'll leave you to get the other four.

At the start of the journey we see No 90583, the inevitable 'WD' in the Gateford sidings at Worksop waiting for an all clear to reverse into Claylands sidings and couple up to a coal train. (27 July 1963)

Class 'O1' 2-8-0 No 63650, with a broken smokebox number plate, is seen near Rotherwood on what appears to be an empty coal train going back to either Beighton or Orgreave pit for a refill. In the distance on the right you can see houses that are situated on the old section of the A57 road to Sheffield. (27 July 1963)

Above left: Class 'EM1' No 26056 *Triton* is parked in the sidings at Rotherwood, one of the most easterly points for the 1.5kV DC electrified line, the other being at Wath. The 'EM1s' and 'EM2s' were the sole operators from 1954 for passenger and goods through the Woodhead Tunnel between Sheffield and Manchester. (27 July 1963)

Left: Class 'EM2' No 27003 *Diana* stands at Darnall just south of Sheffield Victoria, with the crew looking as though they are on a tea break after probably coupling up to the empty coaching stock, indicated by the second man wearing his heavy-duty rubber gloves. What looks like a Chief Mechanical Engineer's carriage saloon is in the siding on the left. (27 July 1963)

Above: Brush Type 2 No D5683 pulls into Sheffield Victoria at 9.15am with a rake of ten mixed coaches, more than likely for one of the many Saturday East Coast seaside specials, as the normal local stopping trains were usually made up of rakes of six. (27 July 1963)

Right: Being pulled by a Class 'EM2' electric, I approach Penistone and just leaving in the opposite direction is English Electric Type 3 No D6742 with more than likely a summer Saturday seaside special, as the headcode includes a 'Z', indicating a special, for example a charter, railtour, etc. (27 July 1963)

Above: Passing Cox & Danks Ltd adjacent to Wadsley Bridge station, you can just make out a Class 'K3' awaiting the inevitable, one of four of the class to be cut up there; this one is likely to be No 61981, as she was cut up in November 1963, the others having succumbed to the cutter's torch before this trip in the early part of the year. According to records, 45 steam locomotives were cut up at this Wadsley Bridge yard, and the most likely outlet for the scrap would have been locally at the Sheffield steelworks. (27 July 1963)

Having gone through Woodhead Tunnel we are now at Guide Bridge station at Audenshaw, where Class 'EM1' No 26016 stands idle; I think an electric was stationed there in case of a failure. The spire of St Stephen's church towers above the overhead wires and pantographs. (27 July 1963)

Class 4F 0-6-0 No 43950, seen near Gorton, is the first steam for about an hour because since 1953 steam had been barred through the 3-mile-long Woodhead Tunnel on the Sheffield to Manchester line. (27 July 1963)

Left: Outside its birthplace, the Beyer Peacock Works at Openshaw, Type 3 diesel-hydraulic 'Hymek' No D7088 has just been outshopped new at a cost of £80,000. Between 1961 and 1964 101 locomotives of this type were produced at the works; the order should have been complete by early 1963 but due to assembly problems at the works they ran 12 months behind schedule. (27 July 1963)

Right: A site plan of the Beyer Peacock works. They closed in 1966 and the boiler shop that can be seen in the left background of the photograph and on the extreme right-hand side of the plan is the only surviving building now on site.

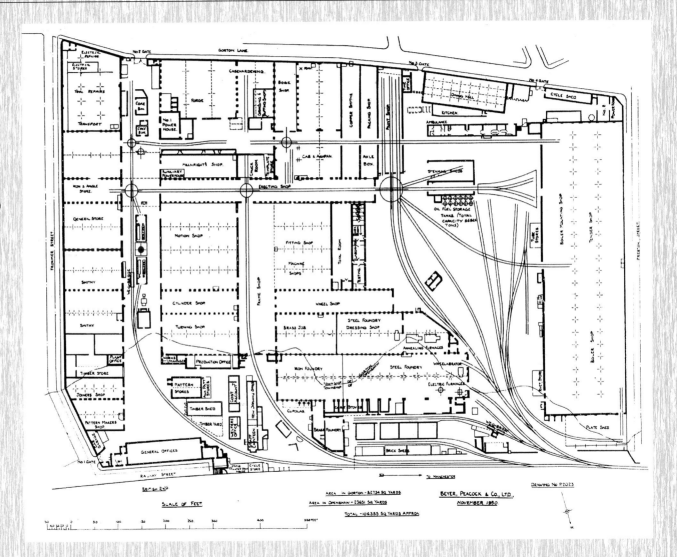

Just past Gorton and close to Manchester are a 'Crab' 2-6-0 and a diesel shunter. The Lowry-esque chimneys of the old mills are evident in the background, together with newer buildings and the shape of things to come at Manchester on the left. I can make out four of the five numbers of the 'Crab' – 4284?. It is therefore fair to assume that it is No 42846, as that was a Gorton locomotive at the time. (27 July 1963)

Above left: Apart from three spotters and two railwaymen, Manchester Piccadilly is completely deserted. The station accommodated two different electrification systems: the line to Sheffield had the now defunct 1.5kV DC system and that to Crewe through to Birmingham and London Euston the 25kV AC system, which prompted the renaming of the revamped station from Manchester London Road in September 1960. (June 1962)

Left: An unidentified English Electric Type 4 pulls away from Stockport displaying the Class 3 headcode of a parcels train heading towards Manchester. Stockport viaduct has 27 arches and stands 111 feet high; built with 11 million bricks, it features in a few of L. S. Lowry's paintings, and from the roads below it dominates the skyline of Stockport. (27 July 1963)

Above: Just coming up to 9B Stockport Edgeley shed, we see Fowler 4MT 2-6-4T No 42374, a BR Standard and a 'WD', with the floodlights of Stockport County's ground on the right – no game today as the season has not yet started. In the middle is the LNWR water tank, and just above the 'WD' is the conveyor belt elevator for coaling the tenders. (27 July 1963)

Above: Dr No, SPECTRE and 007 James Bond – that is what boys thought about when they passed the Lovall telescope at Jodrell Bank, considered to be monitoring the UK's top secrets, counter-intelligence and spies. In those days it was in high-security grounds, but now it is open to the general public as the Jodrell Bank Discovery Centre run by the University of Manchester. (27 July 1963)

Above right: BR Type A electric No E3079, running light near Sandbach, displays the reporting number OZ99 for a light engine, breakdown or overhead line equipment train. Five mature spotters are setting up their camera and tripod and, on the right, three short-trousered ones are apparently floating in the air, well before Spielberg thought of ET – the only ET around was the Electric Traction 25kV AC locomotive! (27 July 1963)

Right: 'Black Five' 4-6-0 No 45351 is on shunting duties at Crewe. It was one of a class of 842, described as a 'do anything, go anywhere' loco, a workhorse of the LMS. On the right is a late-1930s Ford 7Y, probably owned by the original 'boy racer' – it had the factory-fitted option of a single fog lamp, which was only available for the nearside. (27 July 1963)

Right: BR Standard Class 5 No 73048 pulls into Platform 8 from the Chester and Holyhead line with an incredible 21-coach train; it may have been empty stock, though – show off! One spotter has sports jacket, baggy trousers and what looks like a satchel, the other has a jacket, 'drainpipe' trousers and duffle bag – both fairly standard attire for young lads spotting. (27 July 1963)

Left: Rebuilt 'Patriot' Class 4-6-0 No 45526 *Morecambe and Heysham* departs north with an express; although not visible, the train reporting number is 1S91, so more than likely it was going to Glasgow. On the right can be seen the buildings of the locomotive works, just on the junction of the Chester and Glasgow lines. (27 July 1963)

'Black Five' No 44766 is displaying headboard 3K17 but is pulling a mixture of empty stock comprising four coaches, a horse box and a guard's van. The six workmen are seemingly oblivious to the movement, but are obviously feeling confidently safe. (27 July 1963)

At 12.15pm we're nearly finished at the station before attempting the sheds and works. Class 3F No 47677 pulls empty coaching stock out of Platform 3 past the stack of mail bags – I wonder how much money there is in that lot. There must be some – and the getaway bike with derailleur gears is parked at the back of the bags… (27 July 1963)

Left: I'll give it the correct classification now – Class 5MT (but still a 'Black Five'!) No 45276 travels light past the offices of 5A Crewe North. Hopefully in a few minutes I will be in the shed, but well avoiding the offices and the shed foreman. (27 July 1963)

Above: It's about 4 o'clock now and the afternoon shadows are being cast on the tracks from the station canopies. Ten-year-old Ivatt Class 2 2-6-0 No 46516 looks pretty clean, and may have just been in the works for a General; she is now probably going to the South shed and passing two spotters, one of whom appears to be sunbathing fully clothed! (27 July 1963)

Left: English Electric Type 4 No D336, one of Crewe's own, leaves with an express from Birmingham to Glasgow, overtaking three stabled electrics and a GWR 'Hall' Class, which has just pulled in, probably from Cardiff or Shrewsbury. (27 July 1963)

In more or less the same position, after the Ivatt had gone English Electric Type A No E3027 arrived from Manchester with an express for Bristol, with what looks like a non-corridor brake as the second vehicle – pity those in the first corridor coach, as they can't go anywhere! (27 July 1963)

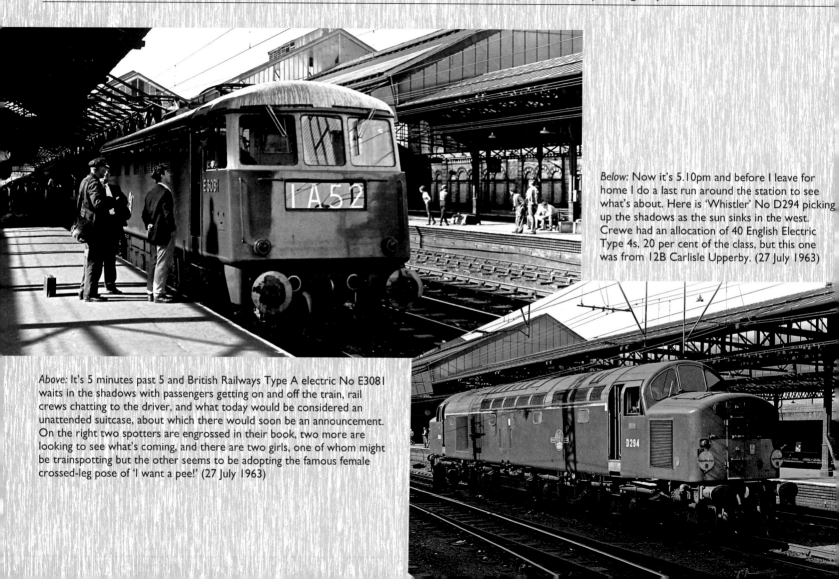

Above: It's 5 minutes past 5 and British Railways Type A electric No E3081 waits in the shadows with passengers getting on and off the train, rail crews chatting to the driver, and what today would be considered an unattended suitcase, about which there would soon be an announcement. On the right two spotters are engrossed in their book, two more are looking to see what's coming, and there are two girls, one of whom might be trainspotting but the other seems to be adopting the famous female crossed-leg pose of 'I want a pee!' (27 July 1963)

Below: Now it's 5.10pm and before I leave for home I do a last run around the station to see what's about. Here is 'Whistler' No D294 picking up the shadows as the sun sinks in the west. Crewe had an allocation of 40 English Electric Type 4s, 20 per cent of the class, but this one was from 12B Carlisle Upperby. (27 July 1963)

7 • Crewe Sheds

This is Gresty Lane – not the venue where Crewe Alexandra play, but the two-road sub-shed of 5B Crewe South, very cramped and never a good spot for a photo. However, it is always good to see a Western engine, in this case 'Grange' No 6839 *Hewell Grange* with the usual work team trying to look busy cleaning out the pit. (June 1962)

I make my way using the quick route past the diesel shed and into Gresty Lane, then cross the main line and drop down into the South shed – perfect! Shaded in the sidings is Class 3F No 47330, introduced in 1924. (27 July 1963)

Above: Another Western Region engine, but this time I am now in the open yards of 5B Crewe South, and posing in a row of out-of-steam locos is 'Grange' No 6866 *Morfa Grange*. The top of the coaling tower is visible on the right. (June 1962)

Above right: 7P 'Patriot' No 45521 *Rhyl* was named after the holiday resort of North Wales. Introduced in 1946, this variant was an Ivatt rebuild of the Fowler originals, with a larger taper boiler, new cylinders and a double chimney. Known to some spotters as 'Baby Scots', I always referred to them as 'Pates'. (June 1962)

Right: 'Jubilee' No 45634 *Trinidad* was a local Crewe South loco, and was withdrawn about a year later, being cut up in Crewe Works, where she was built. (June 1962)

Above: Class 3F No 47450, one of Crewe South's own 'Jintys', is tucked away at the side of the South shed building, but is in steam. (June 1962)

Above right: I have just gone down the alley at the side of house number 39 and entered 5A Crewe North through the entrance at the end of Station Street, to be greeted by 'Coronation' 'Pacific' No 46225 *Duchess of Gloucester* awaiting her next duty. A Fairburn tank, a 'Black Five' and a 'Patriot' are waiting around the turntable, while overhead electrification wires and gantries in the station area can be seen on the left. (June 1962)

Right: Swinging round in the opposite direction in the North shed, with the works buildings in the background, we see 'Jubilee' Class No 45577 *Bengal*, named after what was one of the most densely populated regions on earth and home to the Bengal tiger. (June 1962)

'Britannia' 'Pacific' No 70044 *Earl Haig*, with a slightly different smoke deflector handrail and step arrangement, stands in the yard at Crewe North alongside Standard Class 2 No 78030, both allocated to Crewe North. (June 1962)

Above: 'Black Five' No 45243 is just outside the straight shed of Crewe North; it was one of a class numbering 842 that was built over a period of 17 years from 1934. (June 1962)

Above right: Another local engine in the North shed is Stanier Class 5 No 44763. These 4-6-0s were commonly known as 'Black Fives', 'black' because of the black livery and 'five' from the power classification (5P5F), although I seem to remember that spotters in the Midlands called them 'Mickies'. (June 1962)

Right: 2-6-4 tank No 42213, a 1945 Fairburn development of the Stanier design, poses by the turntable in what was a very full of steam Crewe North. (June 1962)

'Britannia' Class 4-6-2 No 70018 *Flying Dutchman* stands on one of the cramped turntable approach roads at Crewe North. Although now allocated to 9A Longsight, it was one of the original Western Region-based 'Brits' that all had hand/footholds on the smoke deflectors instead of the handrail, which was considered to give better visibility. (June 1962)

Above left: One of the North Wales contingent of 'Black Fives', No 45275 off 6B Mold, awaits her next duty parked by one of the four-road straight sheds of Crewe North. The shed's allocation was in the main for passenger traffic, while the South shed allocation predominantly catered for freight duties. (June 1962)

Above: 'Patriot' No 45512 *Bunsen* at Crewe North. Again, this is a rebuild, but not in the strict sense of the word; they were actually new, but were classified as rebuilds as a paperwork accounting exercise so they could be charged to the revenue account and not the capital account – sounds like a bit of a fiddle to me! (June 1962)

Left: Although the Crewe Diesel Traction Maintenance Depot was open, Crewe North did still play host to diesel locos, and here we see 'Warship' No D839 *Relentless* and two unidentified English Electric Type 4s stabled in the part of the running shed that was nearest the station. (June 1962)

Ivatt Class 2 2-6-2 tank No 41229, 'motor fitted' for push-and-pull working, stands in the yard at Crewe North. (June 1962)

8 • Crewe Works

Above: The normal entry into the Works for spotters was the Eaton Street entrance, but this time I must have gone in through Mill Street because I walked past what seemed to be endless office buildings before getting to the areas that I wanted to see. However, on the way I passed works shunter Class 3F No 47505 standing in the shade. (27 July 1963)

Above right: Another 'Jinty' works shunter simmering in the sun was Class 3F No 47658. She lasted until 31 October 1966 and was then broken up at Cohen's, Kettering. (27 July 1963)

Right: Also on this pleasant walk, which seemed to be miles, was a carriage from the Chief Engineer's Weed Killing Train No 2, No DM198822. Originally built in 1899 by the LNWR, it was in immaculate condition but was apparently withdrawn in 1964 and is now used as a storage shed on a private site near Llansantffraid, Powys; it doesn't look as good as this now. (27 July 1963)

Above: The first glimpse of the real Works was the yard outside the Paint Shops, with two 'Black Fives', No 45417 with No 44938 behind it, just outshopped after an overhaul and paint job. If you were a trainspotter living in that house on Richard Moon Street you would be able to see all the daily activity of locos leaving the works in pristine condition. (27 July 1963)

Above right: 'Black Five' No 44938 was built at Horwich Works in 1946 and is now in Crewe Works. It was eventually withdrawn in 1967; 21 years of age does not seem a lot to me for these wonderful LMS locos. I recall that the guide never took us inside the Paint Shops, maybe because of the paint spraying, but having said that there was not a lot of consideration for your health in those days so I don't know what the reason was – I was too young to question an adult. (27 July 1963)

Right: Class 8F No 48289 stands in the yard on the vacuum pit that was used for steam testing after overhaul; she still has many '8289' identification marks on her body. Two English Electric Type 4s are in the background, while our party of spotters congregates, probably waiting for me to take photos! (27 July 1963)

Class 9F No 92218 stands next to the Brass Finishing Shop. This might have been her first major service, and she is looking as good as new. Built in January 1960 at Swindon Works, she was withdrawn just eight years later – it seems criminal. (27 July 1963)

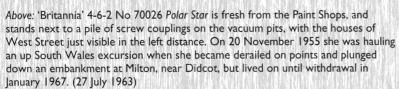

Above: 'Britannia' 4-6-2 No 70026 *Polar Star* is fresh from the Paint Shops, and stands next to a pile of screw couplings on the vacuum pits, with the houses of West Street just visible in the left distance. On 20 November 1955 she was hauling an up South Wales excursion when she became derailed on points and plunged down an embankment at Milton, near Didcot, but lived on until withdrawal in January 1967. (27 July 1963)

Above right: Class 8F No 48256 is another engine parked up after an overhaul and paint job, still with its works identification target number W14 on the frames. Not very often did I see a clean, freshly painted 8F! (27 July 1963)

Right: 'Royal Scot' No 46112 *Sherwood Forester*, without its nameplates and tender, is parked next to Stanier 4MT No 42563, just in front of the new outside traverser that had been installed a couple of years earlier, with the South Erecting Shop on the left. Both locos are finished and immaculate after overhaul, just receiving some final touches before entering normal service. Check out the 'Scot' in the Annesley chapter – what a difference! (June 1962)

This was a surprise for me – 11 'Western' diesel-hydraulics under construction in the Erecting Shop, eventually to be numbered D1035 to D1045. There was no need to check in your *abc* – you knew they were all cops. They only had a short life, some of the class lasting only 11 years; they were considered a non-standard design and most were scrapped. (June 1962)

9 • London

Capital city, the Queen, Parliament, Bank of England, River Thames – what more can you say other than London has nine main-line terminus stations and five main regional sheds. However, if you extended your travel circle, according to the *Shed Directory*'s London itinerary, starting at Old Oak Common and working in a clockwise direction you could visit 14 sheds – but impossible in one day. For my sins, it was a situation similar to the Retford sheds – because I had seen most of the Eastern locos, my main points of interest were the Midland, Southern and Western regions. Consequently there are no photos at King's Cross and I never visited 34A – how stupid was that!

I did not have access to a coloured Underground map, only a black and white one tucked away at the back of my Eastern Region timetable. It was like watching snooker in black and white! Having made the best of the map, my planned itinerary was Metropolitan Line from King's Cross to Paddington, Bakerloo Line to Willesden Junction for 81A Old Oak Common, then 1A Willesden, back on the Bakerloo Line to Waterloo station, a Waterloo local train to Vauxhall for 70A Nine Elms, then finally back to Waterloo for the Northern Line to King's Cross (well, Euston and a little walk), and a 7.20pm departure.

It all sort of went to plan. Old Oak Common was half completed before I saw the police, so I called it a day before they called my time. Willesden was completed with no problem, then it was Nine Elms. The brick-built entry at the end of Brooklands Road had walls about 13 feet high with broken glass along the top and metal signage on either side, in particular one that stated 'TRAIN SPOTTERS ARE PROHIBITED FROM ENTERING THIS YARD'.

'Castle' No 7027 *Thornbury Castle* simmers at Platform 6 at Paddington. A few passengers are walking to the platform exits with handbags, shoulder bags and cases – no sign of laptop computer bags or mobile phones! They're just walking and looking where they are going. The electric truck on the right was used for towing trolleys coupled together. The station is enclosed by the original three Brunel arches built in 1854, a fourth span being added at a later date. Platforms 6 and 7 are now dedicated to the Heathrow Express services. (20 July 1963)

This made me unusually nervous. I don't know what gave me the twitches – maybe I was getting tired at the end of the day. Maybe, when you think about it, it was like breaking out of jail, but you were breaking in, always on the lookout at every corner. Maybe it was the vastness of the depot, with what seemed like very little cover for a trespassing trainspotter. I ended up doing less than half of the shed. I cannot really remember what happened, but probably someone shouted 'Oi, you!' and that was enough for me.

Below: The GWR '1500' Class only comprised ten locos, with about six of them allocated to 81A Old Oak Common for shunting duties in and around Paddington. They were actually route restricted by their relatively high weight, and here the original member of the class, No 1500, shunts empty stock in the London suburbs approaching Royal Oak station; she is just going under the Porchester Road bridge, maybe taking the stock into Paddington station. (20 July 1963)

Above: '5700' Class No 9710, fitted with condensing apparatus specifically for working on the Metropolitan lines between Paddington and Smithfield meat market, waits in the sidings near Scrubbs Lane, Acton, just a few hundred yards from HM Prison Wormwood Scrubs. There are three spotters on the steel-framed access bridge. (20 July 1963)

Above right: Shunting stock in and out of Paddington all day, and approaching Scrubbs Lane road bridge, is clean-looking '9400' Class pannier tank No 8498. (20 July 1963)

Right: 'Warship' No D847 *Strongbow* with another unidentified example behind wait in the approaches to Paddington for their next duty, although they would be 'flying solo', as it was unusual for them to haul trains double-headed. At the time *Strongbow* was based at 83A Newton Abbot, so it is fair to assume that she would soon be on the way home in charge of a service for Exeter or Plymouth. (20 July 1963)

Above: A mixed bag just adjacent to Old Oak Common shed: Class '9400' pannier tank No 9463, a diesel shunter and, on the car transporter, two 1100s and an MGB soft top, together with a fair amount of steam rising to the skyline above Old Oak. Hopefully I would see what was producing it in a few minutes! (20 July 1963)

Above right: No 7034 *Ince Castle* was a newer member of the 'Castle' Class, built in 1950 and based initially at Bristol Bath Road. She transferred to St Phillips Marsh in 1960, then finally in 1961 to Gloucester Horton Road, where she was withdrawn from service in 1965. She is looking in extremely good condition parked in Old Oak Common shed yard, with another spotter on the extreme left walking past the petrol tanker trying to 'bunk' the shed like me. (26 September 1964)

Right: Easily recognisable from a distance, being the only member of the class to have a two-line nameplate, 'Britannia' Class No 70048 *The Territorial Army 1908-1958* was photographed at 1A Willesden shed, which was virtually just across the road from Old Oak Common and was a lot easier to get round. As with most sheds, the drivers, firemen, cleaners and fitters did not seem to be concerned about spotters – they just got on with their duties and we got on with ours. However, it was the man in the blue working coat that you had to watch out for, the blue coat being a mark of seniority – and he usually exercised it. (26 September 1964)

'Jubilee' No 45733 *Novelty* is all coaled up and ready to go, and behind it is a 9F in the yard at Willesden. The 'Jubilees' were a class of 191 locos built between 1934 and 1936 at Crewe, Derby and the North British Locomotive Company in Glasgow; all were named, and half of them were names associated with the British Empire. (14 August 1964)

Above: Four Royal Navy ships were named *Leviathan* – two battleships, an armoured cruiser and an aircraft carrier. All were scrapped, but here at its home shed of 1A Willesden and still intact is ex-LMS 'Jubilee' No 45704 *Leviathan*, coupled to a Fowler tender and hissing steam as she waits for her next turn. (14 August 1964)

Above right: Once a famous class but now just on mundane duties, languishing at her home shed of 1A Willesden is 'Coronation' 'Pacific' No 46240 *City of Coventry*, which looks to be waiting for news of withdrawal; that eventually came two months later in October. (14 August 1964)

Right: Next in the row, with a near identical fate, is No 46239 *City of Chester*, which was also withdrawn in October and cut up at Cashmore's, Great Bridge, in December. (14 August 1964)

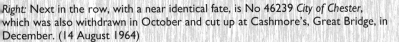

Above: On to 70A Nine Elms now, with 'Merchant Navy' Class No 35019 *French Line CGT* parked near the coal hopper with the driver ready for the off. The depot was closed and demolished in 1967 and the site developed to accommodate the new Covent Garden Flower Market, which opened in 1974 after relocating from its original home. (14 August 1964)

Right: Still at Nine Elms, 'Battle of Britain' Class 'Pacific' No 34059 *Sir Archibald Sinclair* is in steam, with the chimneys of Battersea Power Station just visible behind, which generated electricity until ceasing operations and closing in 1983; after a few aborted attempts, the whole site was eventually bought in 2012 by a Malaysian consortium that had approved planning from Wandsworth Council for hundreds of apartments, offices and shops. (14 August 1964)

Right: 'Battle of Britain' No 34082 *615 Squadron* arrives at Waterloo with the relief 'Atlantic Coast Express' from Padstow. The *Daily Telegraph* advertising campaign appears to be aimed at holidaymakers, boosting newspaper sales by encouraging them to read in a deckchair – unless the cryptic message is something to do with the Cliff Richard film *Summer Holiday*, which was released in 1963… (20 July 1963)

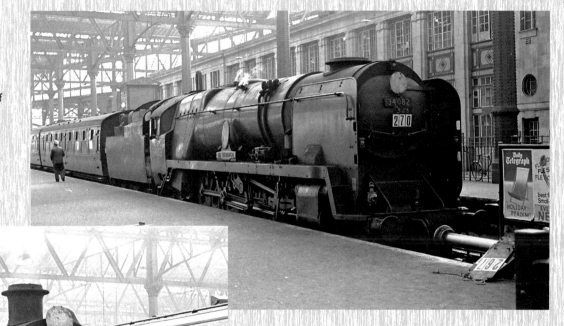

Left: Waterloo with its 21 platforms is the busiest station in the UK, and there were arrivals or departures seemingly all the time, so you had to keep alert in case you missed something, particularly if you collected the electric multiple unit numbers. Platform numbers increased in 1994 to 24 when Waterloo became the London terminus for Eurostar services to Paris and Brussels, but back in 1963, having arrived at Waterloo with the 4.15pm from Basingstoke, is Class 'U' No 31617. Maybe the guards are checking with the driver as to what pub they will meet in later – perhaps it will be the aptly named 'The Wellington' on Waterloo Road just outside the station. (20 July 1963)

Off 71B Bournemouth, 'West Country' Class No 34045 *Ottery St Mary* is due to take out a Waterloo to Basingstoke train, with spotters trying to 'cab' it before departure. The guard has hands on hips, patiently waiting for the 'off' time. In the distance a poster is advertising Battersea Pleasure Gardens – Fun Fair Open Every Day. (20 July 1963)

'Merchant Navy' No 35006 *Peninsular & Oriental S.N. Co* reverses up the line from presumably Nine Elms to Waterloo to take out an express. On the left are the typical Greater London Council flats built in the 1930s, five storeys high with communal open walkways on each floor, while on the right are the new high-rises with no walkways but with internal access and lifts. In the densely populated capital city, where land availability is at a premium, the only way is up, but what then seemed like 'high rise' has now been dwarfed by the newer skyscrapers along the Thames with the regeneration of the old dock areas and Canary Wharf. (20 July 1963)

In 1962 'Battle of Britain' No 34064 *Fighter Command* was fitted with Dr Giesl's oblong ejector, which was a seven-nozzle spark arresting arrangement intended as a solution to exhaust problems; it proved to be a great success, but time was running out for steam, so no more were fitted. Here the loco is travelling light near Vauxhall in an area of what appears to be normal housing, as the roofs on the left are at track level. (20 July 1963)

Above: I am on my way home now, and Brush Type 2 No D5612 is running light on the down line passing beneath Mayor's Walk Bridge north of Peterborough station, which carries the stains of smoke from years of steam locomotives passing through. (20 July 1963)

Above right: In Peterborough New England sidings, one of its own locos, withdrawn and dumped, is 'A2' No 60533 *Happy Knight*, with another 'A2' – a long-wheelbase variant – and two 'V2s'. The 'Pacific' withdrawals were a direct consequence of the closure of Top Shed and the ban on steam south of Peterborough in mid-1963. (20 July 1963)

Right: Class 'B1' No 61273 is in the yards near New England shed, with its coal tower on the extreme left; just to the right, underneath the water tower, can be glimpsed the watering gantry, which was common abroad but rare in the UK. The leather water feed bags were kept hitched up out of the way by a chain when not in use. (20 July 1963)

Class 'WD' No 90169 heads a southbound freight near High Dyke, north of Grantham. On the smokebox door is chalked 'QUO VADIS', a Latin phrase meaning 'Where are you going?' I hope the driver does. I know where I'm going – it's home after a long day at Retford! Coincidentally, No 90169 was off Retford shed. (20 July 1963)

10 • Annesley 16D

Annesley is probably most famous for the flamboyant and romantic poet Lord Byron (1788-1824), who lived at nearby Newstead Abbey. Actually, I have strong connections with him as the pub I lived in was called 'The Lord Byron'!

Nestling in the Nottinghamshire coalfields next to the collieries of Newstead and Annesley, the shed was in the village of Newstead and its engines worked mostly on the movement of coal. The shed was a brick-built six-track dead-end structure that closed in January 1966; it was finally demolished in 1990, its fitting end being buried under a slag heap.

I visited 16D Annesley – one of my local sheds – only once after repeated enthusiastic tales from my mates of how good it was for freight locos and the number that would be on shed on a Sunday. I could not get there directly by rail – it had to be by bus – and I did it on Sunday 24 May 1964, which was a

few days after the Whitsun Mods and Rockers clashes at Margate and Brighton, the Brighton violence being later dramatised in the film *Quadrophenia* (1979).

From memory it was two buses from

Worksop to Mansfield, then change and catch a No 61 Mansfield to Nottingham bus, getting off at Newstead village, then a few minutes' walk to the shed, which was just past Newstead Colliery yard.

Right: Class 'K1' No 62038 from 36A Doncaster was built by the North British Locomotive Company, Glasgow, and according to records its build date was 30 September 1949. It was finally cut up on 30 September 1964 – a nice birthday that was! (24 May 1964)

Above: Another 'K1', No 62013, this time off 36C Frodingham, spent about eight months at Annesley awaiting disposal instructions. (24 May 1964)

Above right: 'K1' No 62032, again off Frodingham, had probably been used mainly for freight to and from the British Steel plant at Scunthorpe. (24 May 1964)

Right: Standard Class 2 2-6-2 tank No 84027 was one of three of the Class 2s that were in later years transferred from the Southern Region to Annesley to work the daily No 5 Link 'Dido' push-and-pull workmen's train from Bulwell to Annesley. It has been suggested that it was nicknamed 'Dido' because it ran 'day in, day out'. You can see the No 5 headboard on top of the smokebox door. (24 May 1964)

Class 'O2' No 63956 had been withdrawn from Grantham and was probably en route to the scrapyard, as it was cut up locally at Rigley's, Bulwell Forest. (24 May 1964)

Having been stored at Carlisle Upperby since October 1963, rebuilt 'Patriot' No 45535 *Sir Herbert Walker K.C.B.* had now been brought to Annesley and was stored there for nearly six months from 29 January until 5 June 1964, then went to Rigley's for cutting up. (24 May 1964)

Right: Class 8F No 48142 was allocated to Annesley with other members of the class in 1962 as a replacement for Annesley's allocation of Class 'O1s', which had been withdrawn en masse at the end of 1962. (24 May 1964)

Below: During the late 1950s 30 9Fs were allocated to Annesley and primarily used on the fast freights to Woodford Halse on the former GCR line, being known as the 'Annesley Runners'. By 1964 the allocation of 9Fs had slightly reduced to 25, and No 92092 is simmering waiting for the next 'runner' duty. (24 May 1964)

Above: 'K1' No 62060 off 50A York looks in excellent condition, unlike the other three of the class we saw earlier. She was in steam and actually lasted until August 1967. (24 May 1964)

Above right: This is Annesley 'Black Five' No 45450. According to Annesley fireman Chris Ward these were the only decent type of Midland engine, being nearly as good as a 'B1'! (24 May 1964)

Right: The first 40 of Class 'B1s' were named after breeds of antelope and eventually nicknamed 'Bongos'. Here No 61030 *Nyala* from Ardsley depot stands on a track just to the right of the coaling tower, which is partially visible on the extreme left. (24 May 1964)

Left: Typical of all of the Class 8Fs on duty five or six days a week, No 48057 was unkempt but still going. (24 May 1964)

Right: 'B1' No 61334 had been officially withdrawn the previous year, in December 1963, and was stored at Annesley awaiting the call from local scrapyard Rigley's of Bulwell Forest for cutting up. (24 May 1964)

Above: 8F No 48141 is parked just in front of a typical Great Central leg crane. In the right background you can see the aerial ropeway that used a bucket system for disposal of spoil at Newstead Colliery. (24 May 1964)

Below: When the Manchester to London sleeper was diverted along the GC line to Marylebone because electrification work was being done on the West Coast Main Line, the 'Black Fives' were used on that service and on other Marylebone semi-fasts. Here is one of them, No 45215. (24 May 1964)

Above: 9F No 92067, looking as though she has worked seven days a week, simmers after more than likely a 'runner' duty. (24 May 1964)

Right: Class 5 No 44846, one of Annesley's own 'Black Fives', went on in service for another four years until April 1968, being broken up at Draper's of Hull. It had nearly made it to the end. (24 May 1964)

A driver's or fireman's eye view from 'Royal Scot' No 46112 *Sherwood Forester* – but she's going nowhere, as there is a telegraph pole in the way. (24 May 1964)

A front view of *Sherwood Forester*, dumped at the end of the road by the crane, never to run again after a collision at Annesley. In the 1960s 15 'Royal Scots' were allocated to the shed, but apparently they were clapped-out examples from other depots, and were brought in to replace the 'Britannias' and also to work the diverted Manchester to Euston sleeper. (24 May 1964)

Index

Silver Link Silk Editions

SLP

In March 2014 we introduced the first of our Silver Link Silk Editions, which will feature a silver, gold or green silk style bookmark (the use of such silks dates back to the reign of Elizabeth 1). Printed on high quality gloss art paper, these sewn hardcover volumes also feature head and tail bands. Such quality and tradition will be much welcomed by today's discerning print book readers.

The Silk Editions are being printed to meet an anticipated demand based on our sales records and experience going back over 30 years. We will be aiming to sell out of each hardback title within six to 18 months thereby making these volumes we believe both collectable and much sought after in years to come. Further Silk Edition volumes will be made available from time to time and details will be shown on our web site: www.nostalgiacollection.com

Further information

Silver Link and Past & Present titles are available while stocks last through bookshops, preserved railways and many heritage sites throughout the UK.

Further details can be found on our web site:
www.nostalgiacollection.com

Our latest catalogue is also available on request by writing to us at the address shown on the title page of this volume or by emailing your request to:

silverlinkpublishing@btconnect.com

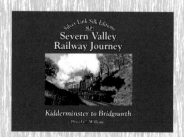

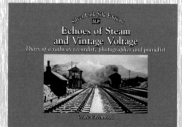